Find Who You Were Born To Be

Explore Your Personality, Discover Your Strengths,

Make Better Life Choices Than Suit Your True Needs

By **Zoe McKey**

Communication Coach and Social Development Trainer

zoemckey@gmail.com

www.zoemckey.com

Copyright © 2017 by Zoe McKey. All rights reserved.

No part of this publication may be reproduced, stored in a retrieval system, or transmitted in any form or by any means, electronic, mechanical, photocopying, recording, scanning or otherwise, except as permitted under Section 107 or 108 of the 1976 United States Copyright Act, without the prior written permission of the author.

Thank you for choosing my book! I would like to show my appreciation for the trust you gave me by giving **FREE GIFTS** for you!

For more information visit: www.zoemckey.com

The checklist talks about *5 key elements of building self-confidence* and contains extra actionable worksheets with practice exercises for deeper learning.

Learn how to:

- Solve 80% of you self-esteem issues with one simple change
- Keep your confidence permanent without falling back to self-doubt
- Not fall into the trap of promising words
- Overcome anxiety
- Be confident among other people

The cheat sheet teaches you three key daily routine techniques to become more productive, have less stress in your life, and be more well-balanced. It also has a step-by-step sample sheet that you can fill in with your daily routines.

Discover how to:

- Overcome procrastination following 8 simple steps
- Become more organized
- Design your yearly, monthly, weekly and daily tasks in the most productive way.
- 3 easy tricks to level up your mornings

TABLE OF CONTENTS

INTRODUCTION 9

CHAPTER 1: THE COUNTERINTUITIVE DISCOVERY OF SELF 19

CHAPTER 2: INTRAPERSONAL INTELLIGENCE 29

CHAPTER 3: THE ATTRACTIVE PERSONALITY 43

CHAPTER 4: WHAT KIND OF TEMPERAMENT AND CHARACTER DO YOU HAVE? 61

CHAPTER 5: PERSONALITY AND WORK 73

CHAPTER 6: OPPOSITES 89

CHAPTER 7: LOVE LANGUAGES 95

CHAPTER 8: IMITATE AND BE IMITATED 101

CHAPTER 9: YOUR PLACE IN THE WORLD 111

FINAL WORDS	119
EPILOGUE	123
REFERENCE	135
MORE BOOKS BY ZOE	137
COMMUNICATION AND CONFIDENCE COACHING	139
ENDNOTES	145

Introduction

There are seven billion people on Earth, and their number is increasing by the day. Although our bodies work on the same biological standards, our minds — and souls — are different. Black or white, short or tall — it doesn't matter. Our bodies function the same way. We need sleep and food, we grow, and we get old. Some aspects of life, the physiological ones, are the same for everyone. But our personalities? That's a different story. We are many, seven billion identities and individual beings. No story is the same, and nobody is worthless or worth less. In a fair world, nobody should feel ashamed of who he or she is. Everybody is unique brain-wise, therefore nobody is unique. In a fair world, we wouldn't care about uniqueness.

But the world is not fair. There are negative feelings and emotions out there like judgment, unmet expectations, guilt, rage, ruthlessness, and shame. We cannot erase them globally with a magic wand. However, we all can take responsibility to work on one individual soul out there. We can make this one person better, aware of his or her worth, satisfied with all the gifts he or she carries. This person is our self.

We can't change others for the better without their willingness. We can guide them, help them, warn them, but when it comes to change, everybody has to make it for him or herself.

We don't think the same way. I know this today more than ever. I come from Europe, a wonderful cavalcade of different nationalities, traditions, and belief systems. Each human is a different world, each country is a separate entity, and Europe is "the old continent."

I often travel to San Francisco, a beautiful, buzzing city that is so different than anything I've experienced before. Everybody is engaged in something purposeful, and the speed of change here is one of a sprinter's. Fitting into the Silicon

Valley atmosphere is quite a challenge for me. I'm very grateful for this challenge, though. It is amazing to see how varied the world can be. I can't wait to travel and see other countries and get to know the habits of other cultures. What are they up to? How do they behave with each other? What is normal there that might be foreign to me?

Sometimes I fear that the western world labels whatever differs from its own dogmas as inferior. Let's take feminism as an example. The first waves of feminism were led by middle-class white women attempting to expand their voice and needs to fight for equal rights. They wanted the same rights for themselves and all the other women in the world. They insisted on the western feminism model, disregarding the needs of other cultures. In the '60s, a new wave of feminism emerged led by other races. They proposed alternative principles, ones which would benefit their lives in their reality. This example strongly illustrates that even if a cause serves a greater good, the concept of good is relative.

There are many layers of good, but we are different. A global greater good would be the disappearance of hunger, something that is connected to our most basic needs.

After the global level, we identify ourselves as a part of a smaller group — part of a nation, a city, or a neighborhood. The best "good" at that level can differ between countries. Our values above the basic instinct level are not identical. Thus it is only natural that our concept of the greater good differs as well. This is where negative feelings start to arise.

When it comes to hunger, the world as one voice expresses regret and dismay. Everybody feels the same way about it. But when we jump a level above basic needs, the voices are not so unified anymore. For example, when communism was collapsing, the capitalist world's tone was unsympathetic and self-righteous. Or when the worldwide financial crisis and the subsequent economic collapse of 2008 began, countries that skewed away from capitalism shook their heads and bemoaned that this was the eventual result of an unbalanced system. There was no "us" anymore, but "they" and "we." We talk about our world and their world, but there is only one world we share.

If we jump to the level of cities, how many cities are in a race with each other? Within a country it often happens that cities are competing with each other to get more financial aid from the government. There is the capital-city-versus-other-big-cities dichotomy. There is a division between one city's football team and another's. People cheering for one team would hate the supporters of the other team. They wouldn't even set foot in that other city if they could help it.

We all are pointing fingers, judging, blaming... We are part of smaller and bigger communities at the same time. There are always expectations that we are supposed to meet in order to qualify as a good neighbor, citizen, countryman, and human. Life always dictates trends we're expected to follow. If your father was a doctor, you should be a doctor. If your town cheers for one team, you cannot cheer for another city's team... and so on.

No wonder we are often afraid to open up in front of our own souls and see what truly lies within. There are so many fixed ideas, identities of who we should be that we rarely dare to be who we really are. If you occasionally feel that expectations overwhelm you and you don't know who you are or supposed to be anymore, that is not proof of your lack of character. It is a common aspect of the civilized human society.

This book is a guide for any person who feels crippled under the weight of expectations to open up and discover him or herself. It's just you and me in a judgment-free zone. Nobody can see inside your head. Time to read empowering thoughts to get some fresh ideas about how to fix and personalize your own little world so that it's best suited for you.

Who am I?

How many times have you tried exploring and getting to know yourself? What kind of experiments have you conducted to get the appropriate answer to this important question?

If you don't have the answer yet, don't worry. Everything that has happened to you in life, all the good and beautiful — or less pleasant but instructive — what you have experienced and lived through so far brought you into this moment. Think of your past as a foundation for the future.

Gone are the days when your parents fed you, bought your clothes, and made sure you got an education (excluding those readers who are still dependent on their parents, of course). Your life was their responsibility. Now you assume this responsibility for yourself. It's no picnic, for sure.

My neighbors had identical twin boys who, even up close, resembled each other like two peas in a pod. As the twins grew, the members of their community admired them. Their parents were very proud of their boys and seized every opportunity to show them off. The kids initially enjoyed their popularity very much, but after a while — after a few years — they had enough of being paraded around and shown off. They were twins, therefore strangers treated them as if their dreams, mentalities, and worldviews would be the same too. But it was far from the truth. One twin was an introverted, reflective, philosophical type of person. The other twin was a party animal, extroverted, and talkative.

Even so, they could switch places from time to time at their school. It was quite entertaining to them to play each other's character. However, if they substituted one another in a situation, the "real" twin failed to experience a milestone life lesson. As they grew up, they understood that the only level to learn life lessons at is the individual level.

How old are you? What happy or sad experiences you have had in your life so far? Do they determine your current lifestyle?

Everyday life is so accelerated. Changes happen so suddenly that it is almost impossible to adapt to them. Many of the accumulated experiences lose their value and it is difficult to rely on them anymore. Seemingly solid points disappear into the multitude of new things brought on by rapid changes. What you believed and trusted in for years can be turned upside-down with each new discovery. Your values are exposed to constant wavering. Therefore, you need to constantly reevaluate the things you have been using as the building blocks of yourself. This is a challenging task — following up the subconscious changes of character. It is almost as difficult as changing the old, ingrained habits. To understand yourself better, you have to keep a mental note of both your changing and static values.

Chapter 1: The Counterintuitive Discovery Of Self

Experts say the borders of the Universe have not yet been found. Since the Big Bang, the Universe has been growing and expanding relative to its center point. In addition, this point, the center of the Big Bang, is not yet known either. The planet Earth is a tiny speck in the Great Cosmos and we consider it our world. The Earth's population is above seven billion people and this number is rapidly growing.

The people of the Earth form their own small worlds in comparison to the planet and all these tiny worlds make up the big picture. We are similar to the components of a huge machine. Each human being has a role in this global mechanism. But from inside out people don't seem to know what their role is. Therefore almost everyone is curious and is searching for something. There are many who want to know why they live and what role they are playing in this comedy called life. People want to explore and learn about their personality, to figure out what kind of job they are best suited for, to see what' written in the stars for them.

Human curiosity and attention is endless when it comes to the central subject of one's own existence — the self. It is not a selfish act to be so self-absorbed, if you think about it. Everybody sees and interprets the world from the inside out. Every minute, every hour, each event you experience involves you. The cars passing before you when you try crossing the road, watching Jack drown in the movie Titanic, embracing your father... all these everyday life events go through your own filter. Whenever you think that you know the world as it is, all you actually know is how you experience it.

I'm stating the obvious here, and I'm aware of that. I'm also aware that these obvious truths are not occupying a conscious spot in your mind. You're not thinking, "Oh, I feel the world orbits around me, but I know that's just because I process each experience internally. Everyone else feels just like I do." Usually you stop at the first part of this thought. I'm not telling this to give you a morality talk. I want to highlight the main reason why you're holding this book.

You wish to discover more about the person you're spending most of your time with. Who forms the opinion of your world "as it is"? It is always interesting to hear stories about yourself told by others — other "worlds" talking about you affords you a feeling of importance, but also a deeper knowledge.

When it comes to self-discovery, we like to listen other people's thoughts about our type of personality. It helps our self-evaluation, creates a deeper connection with ourselves, and grants us perspective. On the other hand, we also like to repel people's opinions if they do not resonate with our own. "I know myself the best," or "I don't need to listen to others' jealousy" — we tend to think this too.

As a conclusion, we can say that we like to hear others' opinions as long as they resonate with our own. When we face criticism, our egos can easily discard it. Only a very few people can swallow criticism without becoming defensive. I'm not talking about destructive criticism, but the genuinely helpful kind.

When criticism hurts, it means it struck a nerve in you. During your experience of discovering the world "as it is," you got wounded. This wound is often not obvious. The best indicator of its existence is your own irritability. Even if you discard the criticism, you won't be able to stop thinking about it. You'll want to know why you received that remark and why you felt hurt by it. You don't know the answer, so you'll turn to external help — personality tests, books, and psychologists. You'll try to get to know yourself better.

Moments of willful self-discovery are some of the few where you're letting your guard down, accepting that there might be a different reality out there besides your own, and for your own protection, you want to know it. When you choose to improve yourself, you unknowingly admit that there is another world out there, one you don't know. Your story still orbits around you, but in a more constructive manner.

There are many life areas you seek information about, not only the painful ones. What job can you best envision yourself in? What do you want to achieve in life? What type of personality do you have? How can you connect your personality to your job, or what's the most compatible personality a prospective partner could have?

There are tests that can give you general guidance about human personality, temperament, and love language types. Based on your answers, they can categorize you into a group that informs you about the general characteristics of that kind of people. But the final answer, as you correctly suggested when you asked why you should listen to others' opinions, is yours.

What do I know about your dreams? What does Gary Chapman, Myers-Briggs, or Freud know about you? We all know scientific research data and numbers, we can provide you guidelines to consider, and general traits that may apply to you, but you have the final word when it comes to choosing a life. (I feel almost gutsy including my own name on that list of greats — Chapman, Myers-Briggs, Freud, and McKey. I should have used them and me. But you get the gist.)

In conventional thinking, the first step in finding out who you are is asking yourself the question and then answering it. I know, it sounds awfully unhelpful. But just like you never actually contemplate your "objective world" being shaped by events where you're always present, you hardly ever answer the question "who am I?" either.

I'll tell you why; it's because usually the question "who I am?" gets followed by another question before it gets answered. Namely, "what's my purpose?" This question is just as hard to answer as the former, so you start jumping back and forth between these questions, trying to explain one with the other.

We hope if we find out who we are, it will actually give us a purpose. Or if we find our purpose, that will illuminate who we are. We get so preoccupied answering these questions that we won't even realize life is passing us by. We'll end up waking with the torment of these questions at the age of fifty, feeling depressed that half of our lives are over and we still don't know our higher purpose, that magnificent aim with which we came to this Earth. It's so inconceivable that after such a long search, such a fierce road of self-discovery, so many personality tests and books, we still don't know how to answer these questions.

But what if we'd asked the wrong questions all along? What if the answer we're looking for does not reside in our 140 IQ, our ENFJ personality type, or our Aries horoscope with an ascendant in Scorpio?

What if the concept of purpose is just as vague and unreliable as believing that your amethyst crystal and your guardian planet, Mars, will send you lots of energy on Wednesdays, but only when it closes a forty-five angle with Pluto?

What if insisting on answering these questions just take us further from the real questions and answers we should focus on?

We have a limited time to live on this Earth. Some more than others, but game over will hit all of us at some point. Between start and game over, we do things. Some of these things are important, but most of them are just time-killers. Even among the important things we do, just a few people achieve executing their important action on a worldwide level. This may sound utterly disappointing, and you may protest, "But I want to hear I'm special and I'm going to make a mark in the world!"

Take a breath, mon ami. Stop getting absorbed by this endeavor. It will make your life miserable.

Whoever we are — or whoever we become — is mostly defined by those important actions we experience during our lifetime. These important events make us happy, give us meaning, and ultimately form who we are.

So instead of focusing on finding a purpose or knowing who you are — in order to find a purpose —try to answer this question:

What are the most important things for me to spend my time on?

This is a much easier question to answer, and with a little contemplation, you can arrive at your conclusion. Weirdly enough, by the time you answer it, you'll get a somewhat clearer picture of the person you are and what you can be good enough at to consider your purpose.

We tend to over-mystify the entire self-discovery process, mostly because of our own self-importance. "This is a life and death question; the answer can't be simple!" Yes, it can, and actually, it is. I know, it sounds insulting in today's culture, where everything from face cream commercials to Oprah enhances individual uniqueness. But the sooner you accept that you and I are not that special after all, the sooner you'll deconstruct that wall of complexity that fosters you from the genuine purpose of human life — happiness. When you start searching for meaning or purpose in the simplest things, you'll be shocked how much you will find.

To procure a breakthrough in self-knowledge, you need to change your current way of approaching the question. For one reason or another, your searching for answers didn't bear fruit until now. Otherwise, I assume you'd know who you are and you wouldn't read this book. If you feel something's wrong with your approach, you're probably right. No matter how well you are doing, how healthy you are, how much love you are surrounded with, as long as you're tormented by the questions "who am I?" and "what's my purpose?" you won't be able to appreciate them. Even if — spoiler alert — at the end of the road, you'll realize that these small things are the true meaning of life.

You can try to change the self-discovery path you're walking on by contemplating on answers to the question, *"What are the most important things for me to spend my time on?"*

Chapter 2: Intrapersonal Intelligence

When it comes to goal-orientation, there are two types of people. There are those who know what they were meant to be since their infancy. My cousin Olga, for example, knew she wanted to be a veterinarian before she knew the alphabet. True, her dream was not impossible-sounding, like saying she wanted to be the first female president of a mildly communist, male-dominated country. Even so, the family didn't take her seriously. Her mother just nodded endearingly, thinking Olga would change her mind when she grew up. Her father didn't even listen when she presented her dream, just reflexively hummed while watching a football game.

Olga was determined, though. Everything she did over the next sixteen years — what she read, the events she took part in, the people she sought — all served her interest of becoming a veterinarian. She finished high school a year earlier than the curriculum suggested and was the youngest person to get a veterinary degree. She could start practicing in a veterinary hospital as early as humanly possible, dedicating her life to healing animals.

People like Olga are the exceptions who empower the rule. There are very few people who know so early, or at any point in their lives, what they want to live for with absolute certainty.

Most of us belong to the other type of people — those who have no clue what to do with our lives. We have lots of passions. We change aspirations more often than Rihanna changes her hairstyle. If you're more like me, you also struggle sometimes to find your place in the world. I had more jobs in the past ten years than I could count on my fingers. I've lived a writer's lifestyle for almost two years now, but I'm still not sure where this career is going or how long I can maintain it. I've gotten a clearer and clearer picture of what I want for my life in the past few months, but it took a long learning curve for me to get here.

A helpful skill for self-discovery

Long ago, we ascended from the level of instinctual life to the higher level of emotional and intellectual life. Now we just have to learn how we can live with ourselves and how we can interact with our environment. This is not an easy achievement. Even though we live in a society that's evolved over the centuries, emotional imprints didn't follow the "human civilization." We still get into emotional WTFs, as I call them. Or "emotional hijacking," as science calls it.

It is a biological fact that our emotional brain (the limbic brain) evolved and learned to function much earlier than our thinking brain (the neocortex). Thus the emotional brain has more power on an instinctual level, reacting more quickly to events. While the thinking brain decides whether or not should you tell you boss he is an old pig with very bad manners, your emotional brain already did the job for you, leaving you in that awkward "did I say this out loud?" moment. Yes, all of us have experienced similar situations when our emotions burst out long before we could judge if it was a smart course of action to take.

Talking without thinking is a typical emotional hijacking moment. Unfortunately, this is not the worst thing that emotional hijacking can cause. Daniel Goleman in his book, Emotional Intelligence, presented a story about a father who instinctively shot his daughter thinking that she was a burglar. The girl was not supposed to be home that night, so when he heard strange noises coming from upstairs, he took his gun with him to check what was going on. The daughter, on the other hand, wanted to scare her dad. When she jumped out from the dark, screaming "boo," her father totally freaked out and instinctively pulled the trigger. The next split-second, his thinking brain overtook his emotional brain and he realized what tragedy had just occurred, but it was too late. In that moment of distress, his survival instinct was stronger than any other thought in his mind. He didn't recognize his daughter's voice, didn't think about the consequences of his action — he purely protected his life, which he felt was in danger.

The unfortunate father's story strongly represents the unpredictable power of the emotional brain.

When you're in a low moment and you think that you don't know who you are, you're not far from the truth. Your emotional brain is so unpredictable that claiming to have a 100 percent self-knowledge would be pure self-deception.

There is, however, a skill — an intelligence, so to speak — that can bring you closer to self-understanding. Howard Gardner in his book, Frames of Mind, presented seven (later eight) intelligence types that humans can possess. He wanted to prove that intelligence measured only by IQ applies inaccurate descriptions to people. If someone doesn't have a high IQ, he might think he's not good for anything. Gardner emphasized in his theory that there are seven (or eight) other intelligence types people can excel at that are just as important as IQ. In my book, Find What You Were Born For, I discuss the topic of the intelligence types in detail. Here I would like to mention only one which is especially important for self-discovery. This intelligence type is intrapersonal intelligence.

Intrapersonal intelligence is the feature of people who can easily detect and understand their own emotions. People have to learn how to cohabitate with the environment and themselves. If they understand their own mind and heart it will be much easier to accept others. Everyday life is strongly influenced by one's intrapersonal intelligence. There's a theory that 80 percent of a person's success depends intrapersonal and interpersonal intelligence. They together make up an individual's emotional intelligence. A well-developed intra- and interpersonal intelligence can remarkably improve personal relationships. Just like understanding our own emotional motivations better can improve our self-acceptance.

People with strong intrapersonal intelligence can be characterized as strong-willed and determined. They know who they are and have high awareness of their abilities. In most cases they have realistic goals. The fact that they have a less biased picture about their abilities gives them an above average self-esteem and self-worth. People with high intrapersonal intelligence are severe self-critics analyzing their actions all the time. They search for rational explanations behind their moods. When something goes wrong in their lives, they go through all the decisions they made. They don't rest until they've found what led them to failure and make a mental note to avoid it in the future.

People with high intrapersonal intelligence are usually psychologists, philosophers, poets, novelists, counselors, or songwriters. Psychology is the typical field where individuals with advanced intrapersonal intelligence are frequently represented. They have an ability to detect, localize, and resolve psychological problems. Most of them chose this path to learn more about themselves, their issues, and then help others with similar problems.

Intrapersonal geniuses are lone wolves rather than social butterflies. They prefer being, thinking, and acting alone. They don't dislike people. They just feel more comfortable inside their own head where they can be in total control. They understand people well, but expressing themselves in company can be difficult. Their communication skills are not as developed as those of people with interpersonal intelligence. They don't chatter, preferring to tell their point as shortly and clearly as possible. They might seem unfriendly and unapproachable, but this is really not the case.

Below are the characteristics that best describe intrapersonal intelligence.

- You have deep self-knowledge, and you're also self-critical.
- You're aware of your own feelings.
- You have a well-developed sense of self and honor your values.
- You have a strong awareness of your purpose in life.
- You have good intuitive abilities.
- You're analytical.
- You are a unique and private person.
- You don't like to go with the flow.

If at least half of the points above apply to you, your intrapersonal intelligence is above average. You can create an unbiased picture of yourself and others easily.

Intrapersonal intelligence is a key need in personal development. The ability to understand your actions better, to become more objective with yourself and control your emotions is part of a healthy adulthood. To develop intrapersonal intelligence you need to practice tracking your thoughts and emotions.

Discover where you stand right now. Identify your values. Think about what motivations lead your life. Identifying values doesn't mean thinking about values like "honesty", "love" and others. You might want to think those are your values but until you find proof in your past that you act upon them, they are just words and concepts. Think back what thoughts and feelings led your latest actions. What where the decisions you made? Do they resonate with the words you claim to be your values? Were you honest or loving?

For example if you'd like to think that you like honesty but you keep lying to people, it means you live in self-deception or worse, you don't act upon your own values. Writing honesty on the paper therefore is lying to yourself or simple bad self-knowledge.

If you realize that you didn't act according to the values you wish to have, no problem. You can correct your behavior. But first you have to identify the bad values you currently act upon. Then change your actions in a way to reflect the values you wish having. For example, if you caught yourself lying often it means that you value easy solutions to problems. You value deception, which grants temporary peace of mind. You value a lack of conflicts. Discover the motivation behind your habitual dishonesty. That is the value you live by today. You can change it if you don't like it.

At the beginning it will be very difficult. You'll feel that you're acting against your current (bad) values. It is only natural to feel uncomfortable when you change something habitual.

Keep a log where you collect your day-to-day thoughts and actions. Periodically check the log to see what changed, what's the same, and what's better within a time period. For example, if you see that you tell the truth more often you're on the good road to change your values for the better.

How to create space for your thoughts?

Find a hobby that sets you far from the crowd. People with a high intrapersonal intelligence are usually introverts. The following saying applies to them: "We have two ears and one mouth so that we can listen twice as much as we speak." Thus they prefer hobbies where they can be alone or where they do not have to interact too much.

This hobby can be just as simple as reading in nature. Find a place where you can be relaxed and get into a meditative mood. Are there any qualities or values you'd like to improve? Collect the benefits of this evolution. Is it worth the effort? If yes, set actionable steps you have to make in order to achieve the desired goal.

Keep a notebook for recording the steps. Every evening write two or three things you have to do the next day to practice the quality you want to improve. Also, write down what you did or did not achieve from the previous day's plan. Think about it. Why did or didn't you accomplish something? How did you feel doing them?

I know this sounds awfully mechanical and troublesome, but our memories are wicked little things. Written words are unquestionable, while memories can "change themselves" with time. The accuracy of your memory might get distorted by your current mood. So, for example, if you are in a bad mood, you might think you didn't achieve anything so far and get melodramatic. But if you check your notes, you'll see the proof that you did many things. You just needed a clear reminder. Help your brain by recording your daily thoughts and actions.

You can try to turn your notes into an autobiography. You don't have to publish it. Just write about yourself in the third person as if you'd write about someone else. Writing (or talking) in the third person always gives perspective, and takes some tension off your shoulders. After you have a few pages in your autobiography, read it. Do you like this person? What do you think about him or her? Would you like to be friends with her? Would you trust him? If you find characteristics you don't like in the person you're reading about, figure out advice you'd like to give to him or her. What would you tell if the person in your autobiography would indeed be a different person? This exercise can help you to stay more objective and less self-hating.

You have the skill to recognize and change your behavior, to build upon your strengths, and improve your character. In our contact with people – in human relationships, in our everyday activities – we need to learn about, handle and manage our emotions, as well as other people's emotions too. The human soul is very complex. There is no universally valid, uniform value scale adopted by the scientific community available to study the human spirit.

Ask yourself the following series of questions.

What is the most important for you? Why are you doing what you do?

Stop reading and analyze what are you thinking about right now? Answer the questions above.

Is what I do now good for me? How does it bring me closer to what I want to achieve and what I want to accomplish? How is it helping me to reach my goal?

Chapter 3: The Attractive Personality

I met the concept of the "attractive character" in Russel Brunson's book, DotCom Secrets. Although his book is about how to upsell products and expand your business, the concept of the attractive character is universal. In Brunson's argument, an attractive character has a backstory, character flaws, identity, stories, and more. Moreover, don't be boring, understand how to use persuasion, and encourage others in their aspirations. Every big movement has a leading figure, regardless of the movement's ethical values. The Nazis had Hitler, Buddhists had Buddha — and these are only two opposing, extreme examples. In order to sell your product successfully, you need followers who will buy it. People like to follow attractive characters, which is why it is so important to become one if you're planning to sell your stuff.

If you want to find who you were born to be and take that something to the next level, you'll need to have an attractive personality. Now I'm not talking about selling something; rather, I'm talking about your specific goal, whatever that is. We live in a human society. Therefore, being likable is a cornerstone of happy, well-balanced life. Everybody likes to be liked. Those who say "I don't care if I'm liked" are usually the most interested in being liked; they just wouldn't admit it.

I'm not saying everybody is obsessed with being liked by everybody. That's not true, of course. But all of us want to be liked by somebody. This being a fact, having an attractive personality is helpful in gaining appreciation, respect, etc.

If you think I'm going to say that in order to be likable, you should smile a lot, be nice all the time, give compliments, and dispense muffins every Wednesday, you're wrong. These are good things, but they won't make you an attractive personality.

The difference between Brunson's attractive character and my attractive personality is that the former can be fake. It exists for the sake of business purposes. It is a mask you don to impress, engage, and oblige your buyers. An attractive personality, on the other hand, is genuine. The main purpose of an attractive personality is to explore and share his or her best self.

An attractive personality is rooted in the idea of self-acceptance. Nothing is more attractive than a human who isn't questioning his actions every step of the road and doesn't get anxious about his own existence, but simply appreciates the time he got to live on this Earth.

I know this sounds awfully simple, but actually, it is the hardest step to take. People think that the hardest step is the end result of figuring out who they are and what their purpose is. These questions are only step two of a much longer process. And as I said in the previous chapters, they are not even the best questions you can ask yourself. Switch them to "what are the most important things for me to spend my time on?"

You see, to be able to select these important activities and spend your precious time on them, first you need to be okay with them. Being okay with them means you accept them. Accepting yourself means that you bow your head in front of your mystery persona, even before you get to know who he or she actually is. This sounds somewhat philosophical, so let me rephrase it.

People fear to accept themselves because it is risky. And we hate risks. Accepting yourself without knowing yourself is like picking up the mystery box from your porch. You didn't order it. It could be filled with candies from a secret admirer, or it could have a bomb ticking inside. It's risky accepting a package like that into your home. You'd rather slam the door on it and go back to watching TV about glamorous stars instead. But the package will still be on your porch. Whatever it contains won't change just because you chose to ignore it. Let's say it is an enchanted package. You can't leave the house until you deal with it. You have two options: taking it in, and in the worst case, learning how to deactivate bombs very quickly. Or you can stay in your house forever, watching the excellence of others on the TV. Oh boy, I think I was too metaphorical this time.

Okay, let me make one last attempt to explain this: if you're a shitty person, you're a shitty person. You'll be a shitty person whether you realize and accept it or you don't. You already are who you are. But unless you accept it, you won't know to truly discover your personality and improve what needs to be improved.

The first step is acceptance.

This is why most self-help advice doesn't work, by the way. They are all built on the assumption that you'll accept yourself first. But that's the twist in almost every person who seeks help — they aren't able to accept themselves. They feel inadequate, not likable enough, awkward, boring, unnatural, annoying, stupid, and so on. They think that first they need to change all those negative feelings to be ready to accept themselves. They are convinced that improvement comes first, then acceptance.

How could this be? If they would accept themselves, why would they need self-help material anyway? That's the goal of most self-help materials — to anesthetize people's pain for a short while instead of curing their problem. The cure is self-acceptance.

You're not awkward

My all-time most-hated word is "awkward." I suffered more from this word in my teenage years than from any other. The school I was studying at boasted a collection of rich kids who considered everything that didn't fit with their rich, local style awkward. Awkward was the synonym for outsider, dumb, disliked, ridiculous, bad, pitiful, and other self-esteem damaging meanings.

People told me I was awkward more times a day than anyone said hello. First I didn't even understand what that meant. At home I wasn't awkward, I was normal. The way I dressed, expressed myself, and acted was normal. In this new school, in this new country, everything I was became awkward. It didn't take me much time to understand the hidden meaning of this word and become utterly self-conscious about everything I was doing. I was terrified to sweat in the summer because "it's awkward." (I don't have to mention that the more I tried to sweat less, the more sweating I did.) I shaved my legs three times so as not to skip even one hair because "it's awkward." I tried to stand or sit so unnaturally cool in order to not be awkward that it indeed became awkward.

I'm sure I'm not the only awkward victim out there. If I could have just one wish, I would eradicate this word and its meaning from the face of the Earth. All of humanity's problems would be solved. There would be no more discrimination or wars because humans wouldn't focus on differences anymore. Awkward, in reality, means different.

I don't like you because your way of being is different than my own, so I hit you with this stupid word to make sure you feel it.

It took me quite a while to overcome the inferiority complex those three years in high school instilled in me. As you can tell based on my passionate opinion about the topic, I'm still not over it completely. But that's fine. I've accepted it. I've accepted that I have this tic I must live with. I fear to be awkward. Counterintuitively, the more okay I am with that fact, the less I care about it.

Did you ever feel inadequate — or worse — were you ever labeled as such? If yes, just know you're not alone. It doesn't matter if you're fifteen, or fifty — the sense of inadequacy can still hurt. The problem of inadequacy is enhanced in today's age of technology. It's never been easier to take individual stories to the masses. Also, it's never been easier to fake happiness. The ideals of perfection are very strong now. There is a clear definition of what it means to be well-dressed, pretty, "a catch," and in good shape. There are also popular opinions out there about everything, which if you don't agree with, you'll be labeled as "awkward."

You can't erase awkwardness, either as a word nor as a concept, from public awareness. Therefore, you shouldn't focus on its elimination. Don't try to convince people that they are wrong or that they hurt you with their scornful remarks. It is not worth the effort. Use this very same effort to ignore them. Every insult only has power over you if you give power to it by believing it, or raging against it.

There are useful, constructive criticisms out there. Awkward (and all its synonyms) is not one of them. As soon as you ignore the awkward label, you'll become more self-assured. Self-assured people are attractive. They are who they are and don't give a flying Fanta about others' disapproval.

Attractive businesses

People don't buy what you do, they buy why you do it. A lot of individuals, service-based companies manufacturing various products are trying to get you to be their customer. There are thousands of them. Yet you still end up talking to a certain agent, contract with only one or two providers and, if you really think about it, you buy certain types of products.

Why is that?

Is your chosen company's product a lot better than the other's? Is their device better, faster or cheaper than their competitors'? What do you really buy when you take your credit card out: a product or a feeling?

The providers producing the best numbers realized that the main goal is not to do business with everyone who needs their service or products but with those who share their goals.[i] Think about the companies, who are leaders in the smartphone market or in IT. There is a lot of competition going on between them. But only one or two end up being really successful. Why? There isn't a big difference between the products of IT companies who are thriving and who are just barely surviving. Why is one more successful than the other?

The decisive factor is how they address their message to their potential customers, us. Salespeople of the unsuccessful companies know everything about the product or service they are trying to sell. They are familiar with all the characteristics, description and operation of their items and still they don't seem to get a major breakthrough in the market. Why is that?

Because they only use the raw, "by the book" sales approach. Most companies fall into this mistake. Certainly it is much easier to teach the technical side of a position. They hire someone who has all the qualifications to be a quick learner. They train this person into an obedient, rule-follower employee and they think they are in business. But the vast majority of people have had enough of aggressive commercials shoving products down their throat.

Creative sales representatives and advertisements of really successful companies bring forth the reason why *they* like the product they are trying to sell you. Besides using these products or services successfully themselves, they can tell you why you should too.

They are able to sell their things to their customers not because people need it, but because their customers feel the same way they do. Companies are on the same wavelength with their customers. So when you buy the product, you don't buy a thing, *you buy an identity*. You buy belonging. You buy a shared value.

If buying an identity applies to tools, it applies to people even more so. Confident people seem much more charismatic and genuinely self-assured with an air of independence. They attract others as berries attract bears — or as blood attracts sharks. It's not about their confidence, per se, but about how they make you feel. Being around confident, charismatic people makes you feel bulletproof too. Being friends with a confident person is like renting a confident identity. Whenever you need a boost, you call the confident friend who charges you.

Those who know less, but are very assured of themselves, do better in business and personal life than those who have a much broader knowledge but struggle with how to make people "buy" it. If people who lack confidence see somebody who has what they long for, they take it as a sign to go for it. They want to relate, assimilate with the confident and self-assured attitude of the attractive personality.

Careful. This might be a slippery slope. If you let your identity be defined by tools or built upon others' confidence, you'll never "find yourself," so to speak. How do you create an attractive personality? Ponder on the following five qualities.

- Discipline

- Patience

- Perseverance

- Resoluteness

- Consistency

- Empathy

Do you have them? Would you like to acquire them? These qualities universally help you to achieve whatever you set your mind to.

Get familiar with your strengths and flaws and accept them. Correct what you dislike. It is always better to accept your flaws and be comfortable about them than try to hide them. Everybody has flaws, thus nobody can truly relate with a "perfect" human. You may think that an attractive personality is built for the outside world – to find your place easier among others and meet others' expectations. This is not the reason, but the result.

The reason to have an attractive personality is to feel internally comfortable. It's not a mask, but genuine self-acceptance.

Do you remember how many times you were asked as a child, "what and how do you want to be when you grow up?" I am sure you had a few ideas about what you wanted to become, talking about them all starry-eyed and enthusiastic. What changed in you since then?

You have learned, seen and experienced a lot over the years. You have confronted situations you were not prepared for. You are not even conscious of the results and the impacts of these events on your life. You've got everything – stored in your subconscious – that is necessary for a restart.

How do you build up the person you want to become?

Make a list of the most important and common qualities you know — every quality you admire and value, or dislike and resent. How will you discover yourself among these qualities?

Put a tick next to each quality, good or bad, that you think you own. Write a plus sign next to the qualities you think you don't have, but you wish you did. Write one minus sign next to that ticked bad quality you wish to eradicate from your life the most.

For example:

Beautiful +
Smart ✓
Considerate
Good listener +
Selfish ✓
Charismatic +
Resilient ✓
Resourceful ✓
Mean
Oblivious ✓ -

This list is not exhaustive by far. You can write down dozens and dozens of qualities. The more qualities you write, the more accurate of a picture you get. Be honest when you tick the qualities that describe you. If you are not honest, you will give answers that make you appear in the best light – or the worst. Your responses will be biased and very far from reality. Don't waste your time on self-deception. So get over the "first date syndrome" where you usually present your best side.

Ask yourself four simple, but important, questions. Answer them honestly.

> a) How did I want to be when I was young? What do you remember from the period before you were fourteen years old?
>
> b) What was I like and what kind of self-image did I have five to fifteen years ago?
>
> c) What am I like and what kind of self-image do I have now?
>
> d) What do I want to be like and what kind of self-image do I want to have in five to fifteen years?

Under all four questions, list five to ten parameters, attributes, skills, strengths, or talents that best define your status in that period, then rank them according to importance, relevance, and efficiency. List the parameters you gave as an answer to each question from one to ten based on your current values. Write the ranking in a column for clarity.

For example, you answered question a) with the following qualities: curious, adventurous, daring, popular, fast-thinker. This is my top-five quality chart based on my fourteen-year-old or younger character assumption. Based on my current values, I would rank them as the following:

1. fast-thinker (the most important)

2. curious

3. adventurous

4. daring

5. popular (the least important)

I can't tell how would I have ranked these qualities back in high school — being fourteen years old — but I have a strong feeling that number one and five would be switched. Collect the qualities to answer questions a), b), c), and d), and do the same thing I did with the ranking.

In half a year, one year, five years, or even ten years, open the folder of this exercise and repeat it. Your perception might have changed about the qualities and the ranking as the years passed. Keep track of it.

This is a long-term project, but it is an accurate indicator of character change. You can track whether you indeed improved in the direction you wished for five years ago. You can also see how your values changed. For example, in five years, my ranking of the five qualities above would look like this:

1. adventurous (the most important)

2. daring

3. fast-thinker

4. curious

5. popular (the least important)

Who knows what the future brings? But completing and keeping your results of this exercise will help to recall where that future stems from.

Chapter 4: What Kind of Temperament and Character Do You Have?

As you could deduce from my first chapters, I'm a big fan of self-questioning. There are, however, some personality studies that are worth knowing. Information offered by psychological discoveries such as temperament types, love language types, and personality types teach us valuable lessons on what kind of questions we should ask ourselves. In the following chapters, I will talk about the most successful personality tests, studies, and research.

What type of person are you? Are you hotheaded or laid-back? Knowing your basic temperament can help you a lot in life. The more you know about your natural temperament, the better you can choose your profession and hobbies. Also, the more you can control it. People often shrug it off, "That's how he was born. He will do well in life."

Or "He won't be anything but a slacker." Partially is coded in your genes, that certain something that defines your personality. Partially it is up to you.

If you see or hear someone obnoxious, are you ready to ritually sacrifice them? Why is that? Because you were born this way, or because your environment taught you to do so?

According to a psychobiological model developed by the American psychiatrist Robert Cloninger, personalities are determined by how differently they adopt, store and process information.

Cloninger's personality model tries to integrate the standard personality variables, psychiatric disorders, neurobiological mechanisms and learning theory into a biopsychosocial theory. In his theory, learning, social, genetic and biological variables are considered equally important. He approaches the concept of personality from two sides, temperament and character.

Temperament signifies the differences manifested in auto-responders given to emotional stimuli, and these are largely inherited, relatively independent of the environment. Underlying the temperament factors, Cloninger assumed processes regulated by the brain.

He differentiated four temperament dimensions, which represent the four main dimensions of automatic responses given to stimuli perceived. It shows the individual differences in the area of associative learning with responses to novelty, danger, punishment and reward.

Character means the set of concepts we have for ourselves, for others and for the world. In other words, while temperament determines the basic emotional responses, habits and moods, character influences intents, goals and attitudes. Temperament means predispositions defined at birth. Character, on the other hand, shows what someone can intentionally actualize. The development of character takes place during socialization, through the effects of socialization to the individual.

The whole personality is determined by the temperament and character together. Temperament influences the development of the character to a certain point, but it does not determine it. While we can draw conclusions to a person's predispositions from his temperament constellations, character constellations are influenced by socialization and socio-cultural learning. [ii]

Over time, a trend emerged, namely the categorization of people from a psychological point of view. If we understand and recognize the differences between different psychological categories, we can better comprehend the communication between people and the motives behind the behavior of our surroundings. Each temperament type is characterized by different behaviors and all have similar traits.

- Traits of melancholic type: talented, creative, analytical, idealistic, pessimistic, masochistic, critical and uncertain.

- Traits of choleric type: a born leader, dynamic, independent, self-sufficient, impatient, manipulative, unable to relax, overly dominant.

- Traits of phlegmatic type: focused, relaxed, sympathetic, avoids conflict, selfish, avoids responsibility, worrier, self-righteous.

- Traits of sanguine type: vibrant, sociable, open, talkative, naïve, loud, always exaggerating, undisciplined.

According to Jung, there are two types of personalities, extrovert and introvert.

People with sanguine and choleric temperaments are usually extroverts. They are the ones who use their energy on the subject and put the emphasis on action or people. Their goal is to change the world.

Melancholic and phlegmatic people can be described as introverts. Their subjects are deprived of fervor. They are forced to conserve, to reflect and to think through almost all their actions, so they are slow. At the same time, they are fearful and shy too. They constantly try to adapt to their environment.

Extroverts are tempted by everything that's new and unknown. They act first, then analyze. Their actions are quick, without hesitation. No consideration, no slowing down.

Who are you most similar to?

In ancient times, Hippocrates and Galen were contemplating the idea of classifying people based on their personality traits. They named the four temperaments after the four elements: fire, water, air and earth. These elements stand for choleric, melancholic, sanguine and phlegmatic based on what they thought were the predominant bodily fluids.

Major changes have occurred in the 20th century in the field of personality psychology influenced by the Swiss-born psychiatrist and psychologist Carl Gustav Jung, and Erick Jaensch and Kretschmer. Their impact is felt in some notable researchers' personality tests, who conducted their research based on their theories.

A questionnaire called CPI (California Psychological Inventory) is a test made up of 480 yes or no questions, published by Harrison Gough (1956). It is similar to MMPI (Minnesota Multiphasic Personality Inventory) test, because out of 480 questions they included 194 questions right from MMPI. If you are interested in getting to know which general criteria of personality you fall into, take these tests. These tests are similar to the tests that are used for job interviews.

Temperament test

To make it easier for you, I "stole" the personality test off the website of my University's student organizations. You can find the link in the Epilogue part of the book. However, if you don't speak Hungarian, it won't be of much help. Here, however, you can find the test in English, translated by myself.

Write the following letters on a piece of paper: S, M, C, P. These letters are the abbreviations for sanguine, melancholic, choleric and phlegmatic.

Read through the statements below. If one is true, mark it next to the corresponding letter. At the end of the test count how many check marks you have next to each letter and click back to the Personality Types chapter.

S   1. People say I'm very friendly.

M   2. I only have a few friends, but we are very close.

C   3. I am a born leader.

P   4. I'd rather save money than spend it.

S   5. I enjoy life.

M   6. I love it when every detail is perfect.

M   7. I never know what kind of emotions will rule my day.

M   8. I find it easy to criticize people.

C   9. I have an explosive temperament.

P   10. It is hard for me to make decisions.

P   11. Nothing really bothers me.

S   12. I often exaggerate.

S   13. I am not very trustworthy.

M   14. I am very self-disciplined.

C   15. I am often cold and indifferent.

C   16. I am determined.

P   17. I have a dry sense of humor.

P   18. I like just hanging out, doing nothing.

S   19. I am absent-minded.

P   20. I'd rather spectate than participate.

C   21. It is hard for me to forgive.

C   22. I am very active.

S   23. Sometimes people say I am very loud.

M   24. I tend to be pessimistic and negative.

P   25. I am not energetic.

P   26. I am very patient.

S   27. I like to talk.

M   28. I don't like big parties, and I prefer being with a few close friends.

S   29. I am enthusiastic.

C   30. People say I am very brave.

C   31. I have an opinion about everything.

P   32. I like to sleep a lot.

C   33. I like to keep situations and people under my control.

M   34. It is difficult for me to make friends.

M   35. I love music and arts.

S   36. I like almost everyone.

C   37. I am very confident.

M 38. I often think people don't like me.

S 39. I am generous.

P 40. I often feel tired.

When you are done, go to the Epilogue and read the description of your temperament type.

When you are done, go to the epilogue and read the description of your temperament type.

To develop this idea further, I have a suggestion for you. One afternoon, invite your best friends over for tea or call your spouse and child for a fun family program. Take this simple test above and do it three times, first for yourself, then for the person sitting on your left, and lastly for the person sitting on your right, or vice versa. If you are more than three, do the test for each person present. It is very interesting to see how you characterize yourself versus the people who are closest to you. If the answers overlap, there is a good chance you know yourself quite accurately and you open up to your friends honestly. If there are little differences, your friends can help you clarify the gaps you have in your self-knowledge.

A three-dimensional picture of your temperament will thus be created from your and your friends' perspectives. Don't tell them what to expect, otherwise they might become biased to appease you.

Chapter 5: Personality and Work

The environment you live in, the opportunities of the place, and the economic and political situation often determine the source of your livelihood. Consider the following sentences and think about them when you are stuck.

Do you like what you are doing or are you doing it just to make a living?

Do you think you must have extraordinary talents and special abilities to get somewhere in life?

What do you need to get by?

My father used to tell me "whatever you do, do it with 110% devotion. Give it your all, be the best, even if you are a street-sweeper." In the beginning, I doubted him. I thought this was one of those cliché sayings that people used just to say something motivating. Recently I realized that he was right. I was working in a very comfortable manner. I read, wrote, designed, and managed my business in a half-assed manner. I delivered the bare minimum I expected from myself, but nothing more. This lukewarm existence didn't make me a better person, nor a happier one.

Failure is the best teacher. I failed. Again and again. I failed, collected my will, and did my job with 110% dedication, but when I reached my goal, I let my work ethic loosen again. And again. I thought I'd learned from my past mistakes, but I proved to myself repeatedly that I hadn't. Here's the other cliché: "Learn from your failures." I tried to learn, but I didn't. Every time things started to get a little better, I became comfortable again with jumping off the treadmill and nesting myself into the velvet throne of idleness.

Why do I do this?

In most cases, I'm aware of self-sabotaging. I think about it day and night, wondering why I can't force myself to do what I know I have to do to progress. Have you ever experienced this feeling?

If you're human, I'm sure you did at some point in your life. Let's call this feeling by its real name: procrastination.

You don't know it, but three days have passed since I wrote the previous sentence and this one. I procrastinated on writing this part of the book on procrastination. In these three days, I watched thirty episodes of Tom & Jerry to relive my childhood, cleaned my microwave, re-organized my dresser, fixed the pigeon-repelling owl on the balcony, and went for double Zumba classes.

Why is this still happening? Why can't I just write this chapter in one sitting and get over it? I feel the topic itself is dragging my productivity in the mud. But even the mud is better than sitting in front of the computer. So I rolled and rolled in the mud in the last three days, pondering on my own laziness, hoping to come up with a magical solution for you. I didn't debug one of the biggest mysteries of humankind — how to defeat procrastination.

There is no magic formula to defeat procrastination. Whatever we procrastinate upon is not important enough in the moment of procrastination. Even if it is, it isn't. Completing the task you're procrastinating on would bring your some satisfaction, some happiness — some good feelings, generally. But you have strong negative feelings attached to the action in question, as well. As long as the negative feelings (sloth, fear, distractions, insecurity…) overthrow the positive, you'll keep procrastinating.[iii]

As soon as the pressure on you grows to an unbearable level and avoiding the task will incur worse consequences than just doing it — that's when you'll take action.

There are some tricks I use to kick myself into a productive mood quicker than if I let my procrastination go away organically.

The easiest but often most efficient solution for me is to work close to a hard-working person. Once you see somebody being crazy active and productive next to you — if you're anything like I am — you'll feel embarrassed by your own idleness and you'll start doing something. That little something will oil the wheels of activity. Before you know it, you'll be deep in your work.

It doesn't matter what your goal is — find somebody who works on it as you would like to work. For example, if you want to lose weight, go to the gym with one of your gym rat friends. If you want to study, hit the library with a bookworm. If you want to practice your speech, team up with somebody who is keen on public speaking.

If there is absolutely no motivational person around you, there is another trick to beat procrastination. Namely, start doing something. Something small and simple. For example, when I have zero motivation to write, I start reading blogs or books, taking notes, elaborating on those notes, writing my impressions about the thoughts in my idea file. The ideas start to grow detailed. They create a paragraph. Before I notice it, I have already written a chapter. The key is that I don't tell my brain, "Hey, brain, now you'll be physically glued to this chair until you finish two thousand words." No, I just lure myself to the table like you lure a cat out under the bed with a slice of ham. "Come, now. We're going to read a little bit now. Good. No need to worry, it's just for twenty minutes. Sit here, read this. The faster you do it, the quicker you escape."

If there are legitimate explanations for white lies, there should be some for white self-deceptions, too. For a good cause, you can trick yourself into productivity. Of course, nothing is foolproof. You might not get engaged in whatever you tricked yourself into doing. In this case, you finish your twenty minutes of reading and go back procrastinating. Even so, at least you did something for twenty minutes. This way, you have a chance to get engaged in what you're doing and get productive again.

If you understand why you procrastinate, you'll know yourself better

People tend to think that procrastination is rooted in one simple feeling: laziness. This may be shocking, but the main reason behind procrastination is not laziness, in most cases. When you're procrastinating about taking out the trash or washing the dishes, indeed laziness is the main de-motivator. You won't take action until your house starts smelling like rotten meat and potatoes, or you run out of mugs to have your morning coffee in. Deep down, you know trash will smell sooner rather than later and that you have only five mugs to drink from, but the situation is not urgent enough until your thoughts become reality. As soon as the reasons to take out the trash overthrow the reasons to wait, you'll get up from your couch and drag the smelly beast at least out to your porch. Then you grumpily wash at least one mug of the five you have for your coffee.

Tasks like these are mundane and dull, and it is obvious why you procrastinate. The tricky questions arise with the more complex issues you procrastinate on, like breaking up with your partner, finding a new job or quitting a job, changing business fields, investing in bitcoins, having a heart-to-heart conversation with your kid about sex, and so on. On tasks like these, you may procrastinate big-time — for weeks, months, even years. If you don't take this kind of procrastination under profound self-analysis, it might last a lifetime.

You may know that breaking up with your partner would be the right thing to do for both of your sakes, but you feel too scared to be the decision-maker. What if it is the wrong decision? Let him take on the responsibility. Or you know you won't get any younger and the more you delay changing jobs, the less of a chance you'll have of getting hired. But what if the new job is even worse than this current one which I know inside-out? Or you know your money doesn't earn for you just sitting in a bank, or worse, in your piggy bank at home, but you're too afraid to risk investing it. Decisions like these generate a lot of emotional distress and internal struggle. As a defense mechanism, you try to find excuses to not do them.

I'll just wait one more month to see if we'll get happier.

I'll just wait until the next quarter. Who would want to leave before getting a bonus?

I'll just invest in bitcoin the next time the price is low.

Procrastinating on a life-changing event is always rooted in some kind of fear. You may tell yourself that you're lazy, or cautious, or just too comfortable, but the truth is that you're afraid. Of failure, or even of success. Of being alone, or of leaving someone else alone. To lose your money. You name it. Sometimes you can be conscious about your fears, but most of the time, you don't realize they are keeping you stuck.

So where is this stupid fear coming from? How can you handle it? How can I handle it?

I found the answer to these questions in a very unexpected place: a blog post. I read about procrastination in a blog post of Mark Manson's where he elaborated on a new law he'd invented. He called it Manson's Law, and he has come up with similar laws like Parkinson's Law, which states that "work expands so as to fill up the time available for its completion," and Murphy's Law, which states that "whatever can go wrong, will go wrong." Manson's Law states that "the more something threatens your identity, the more you will avoid doing it."[i]

If you struggle with figuring out who you are, just take a mental note of the things you're avoiding and procrastinating on. These things probably threaten your identity. Therefore, your identity is the opposite of the things you're trying to avoid. Tada! It's a very easy way to engage in some self-discovery thanks to procrastination.

Even if you don't know your limits, you have an image about yourself. Anything, good or bad, threatening that image becomes a potential reason for procrastination. Manson mentions that making a million dollars or losing all your money can equally threaten who you are.

Oftentimes, we're not afraid of the negative. We're afraid of the unknown.

This is why people are afraid of success — subconsciously — just as much as they fear failure. Because they don't know what success holds for them.

You fear to do kinky stuff with your spouse, even if you want it because it threatens your "good girl" identity. You fear to do something innovative at your workplace because it wouldn't fit in with your precise, follow-the-rules persona.

Do you have a book you've written and perfected for five years, but have never published because it's not good enough yet? And maybe because you're also a nurse, and nurses don't know much about book writing?

Whether or not you think you know yourself, you have a belief about who you are. You have the identity of the nice guy, the mean girl, or something else. These identities are conscious, so you'll directly avoid situations which contradict your character. People also like to validate their beliefs, so if you think you're a mean girl, you'll engage in activities that prove it again and again.

Identities and fears are strongly connected. A perceived identity grants perceived security, so doing something contradictory evokes a lot of emotional resistance. You don't settle with one man because you fear it will threaten your independent girl image. You don't move away from your parents because you fear you'll fail running your own household and you'll have to go back. As long as you stick to a perceived identity, you will face procrastination again and again.

Okay, so what should I do? Be more positive?

Not quite. According to Manson and other thinkers, positivity can get you stuck just as much as negativity.

"The more I think about how amazing an article I'm going to write is going to be, the more I procrastinate and the harder it is to write it. Conversely, when I stop caring whether the article is great or not, the article feels as though it 'writes itself' and it usually turns out great," Manson confessed in his post.

I noticed the same thing going on when I wanted to be a good, exciting, smart, witty, slutty, everything girlfriend for my man. I was so self-conscious not being good enough for him. I spent hours and hours thinking about what I should say, how I should move, how I should dress, do my makeup, and how I could be better at making out with him in order to be the best partner. The more anxious I got, the less time I wanted to spend with him. I didn't want to mess up anything, and the more we were together, the more opportunity there was for a fiasco. One day he told me I wasn't challenging enough and he felt that all I did was please him. I was shocked. I'd put all that effort into being perfect for nothing? Did I make things worse?

After I recovered from that wound, I started not caring. The less I cared, the more interested he became in being around me, and weirdly, the better girlfriend I became. This happened years ago. Since then, our relationship is doing very well. I care about him, of course, but not at the expense of my own interests. I tell him if I don't agree with something or if I don't want to eat Vietnamese again. He gets it, and he respects it.

I'm sure you've experienced in some area of your life the surprising benefit of not caring too much. If you care too much, you'll get frustrated, anxious, and enslaved by your high hopes. If you care less, you'll just do stuff organically without any "what ifs" or stress involved.

The higher the expectation, the more intense the procrastination. If I wanted to write the best book ever written on this planet, I'd probably die before even trying. If I just wanted to write a good book, a helpful book, not too fluffy, just to the point, involving my best knowledge, and there were no other consequences beyond some bad reviews and poor sales, I'd procrastinate less than a day.

If you're too optimistic, too positive, possessed of a "yeah, yeah you can do it, yeah" attitude, you'll end up crumbling under that tremendous amount of awesomeness you put on your shoulders to live up to. Unless your identity is to be the most amazing walking-talking human on Earth, you will feel threatened deep down by failure and you will procrastinate.

To escape long-term procrastination needs more action than just overcoming sloth. You'll need to identify the fear behind the procrastination. Identifying the fear will shed light on who you are — if you feel threatened by something, you probably are the opposite of that something. Carefully examine what stories you tell yourself about your identity and what the goals or changes are you'd like to make to improve your personality.

But how can I improve? Knowing the whys is not helping.

The how is very simple: Stop caring so much, even about the perceived identity you have. That perceived identity is nothing more than a bunch of stories you told yourself about who you are and believed in. These stories, however, are far from reality. If you accept that you actually have no idea who you are, this acceptance will open many doors for you to change and grow.

Do you stick to the image of the unerring businessman? If you admitted that you made a mistake in your calculations because you're a human and not a robot, you'd free yourself from the struggle of being without error all the time.

When I admitted to myself that I don't have the high-achiever American spirit my boyfriend is used to, but I still have my values for which he chose me in the first place, I felt free to be sassy, adventurous, sometimes overly naïve and careless again. I didn't force myself to become somebody I thought Silicon Valley women were. And it worked out for the best.

Even though we perceive the world differently and we have our own personalities and souls, our problems are very similar.

Try this counterintuitive approach. Instead of trying to be special at any cost, try to be who you are in the moment: a wife, a father, a daughter, a friend, a nurse. It sounds lame, but it is extremely liberating to know that you don't have problems so unique that people could never conceive of them. Earth-shatteringly high expectations create equal amount of stress and compulsive compliance. And fear and procrastination, of course. Your grandiose ideas of self are the ones which hold you back.

Ironically, the world's best sportsmen and women and other high-achievers think of themselves as awfully average, or even below average. That's what pushes them to do whatever it takes to improve day by day. They know that a drop of rain can wash a mountain away with persistence, patience, and discipline.

Chapter 6: Opposites

It is time to take a look at a more mundane way of getting to know yourself. The Business Insider published an article about what type of work suits different personality types. The Myers-Briggs Type Indicator (MBTI) personality test has been used in the business world for decades. Eighty% of Fortune 500 companies use this test for their new recruits.

The test determines sixteen personality types and — although the list is not definitive, as personalities can change over time — it can provide interesting insights as to what type of work one should choose.

The test categorizes people into the following eight personality preferences: introversion, extroversion, thinking, feeling, judging, perceiving, intuition, and sensing.

For example, introverts in the sensing group and people with a preference for judging would do well as accountants, web developers, auditors, or in governmental positions, according to the test. On the other hand, someone who is introverted with a preference for intuition, perceiving, or feeling could be a good psychologist, writer, or could work in HR.

When using the introvert-extrovert paradigm in everyday life, we usually mean someone who is little aloof versus someone sociable. This statement is overly reductive because it jumps to a conclusion based on only one personal characteristic. The MBTI measures behavioral preference, which is not the same as a person's character. Character is static, more set into one's mind. Character identities can be quite influential and hard to differ from, as we saw in the previous chapter, whereas many events can influence behavior. We can say behavior is dynamic. In the original Jungian theory, the dichotomy of character and behavior is meant to characterize the source of spiritual energies: introverts' energy comes from internal sources, while extroverts' energy comes from external sources.

The sensing-intuition dichotomy: people belonging to the sensing group are more sensitive to concrete phenomena or, in other words what they can sense from outside, while those who prefer intuition are more receptive to correlations, which are associations gained from information from the outside.

The feeling-thinking dichotomy: those who feeling deeper listen to their instincts. The thinkers strive to find logic explanations rather than emotion-based ones.

The judging-perceiving dichotomy: people with the preference for judging like to have things clearly categorized so they can make quick decisions, while this is not the preference of perceivers. They are the ones who interpret or look on someone (or something) in a particular way.

Extroverted people (E-type) are able to take on a lot of information from the world, but they often treat and process it superficially compared to introverts. Extroverts get their energy from the outside. They make friends easily and have a lot of relationships but often these are one-dimensional.

They are talkative, highly communicative. Usually they think while they talk or after. Not before. They perform well in areas where they can talk and express their emotions, even if those emotions don't really exist, like acting and politics. They get along in the world just fine. They are usually cheerful in their social interactions but this is often just an appearance. In reality they have just as many problems as introverts, but it is easier for them to ask for help.

It can be bothersome that extroverts can be superficial oftentimes and talk a lot without a purpose. Their self-revelations and their need for others to do the same sometimes grossly violates other people's intimate spheres, without them being aware of it.

They want an immediate response to their questions, seem impatient and sometimes they are impatient. They are not only happy to work with others, but actually prefer it. For extroverts it is difficult to work alone. They need constant company, social interactions and events otherwise they become bored quickly.

Introverted people (I-types) get their information through a much narrower channel than extroverts despite (or perhaps because of) the information obtained is much more carefully processed and internalized. They are more cautious and thorough with the stimuli they get from the world than E-types. They get their energy from their own internal world.

It is difficult for them to make connections but, if they succeed, their friendships are much deep and honest. They can seem quiet and disinterested, even rude because of their silent withdrawal. They don't immediately respond to questions and problems. But this is a sign of internal processing. They are not slow, indifferent, or unfriendly. When they speak up they have just as good, if not more meaningful things to say than an extrovert. They can better express themselves in writing, perhaps because this form of communication is slower.

What do you think? Are you a more introverted or extroverted person? I'm sure you have an idea about this answer. But do you know if you're more intuitive or more sensing type of person? Or more judging than perceiving? Following the link you can fill the Myers-Briggs Type Indicator for free: https://www.16personalities.com. Discover which general personality type defines you the most. Even if you pick a different test to find your personality type I would suggest taking your time and doing one of the longer ones. Those give a more accurate response.

Did you do the test? What do you think about the personality description? It is never too late to learn something new – even about yourself. If you let go of enormous expectations, and stone-carved identity beliefs, you can become like an empty book having lot of space to fill with new things.

Chapter 7: Love Languages

Have you heard about the concept of love languages? Did you see that cheesy purple-covered book topping the charts of Amazon's Family and Relationship book category? Or in a bookstore? Or anywhere?

Many people must have heard of them, whether as a well-informed woman or as the partner of a well-informed woman. Gender stereotypes aside, women are more interested in reading about love-related stuff. But here's the catch — Gary Chapman's book is not smellier than blue cheese. Actually, he makes a very logical and sensible point with his five categories on love languages.

Gary Chapman, the writer of the book The 5 Love Languages and an American family counselor, has conducted more than thirty years of research on this particular topic, which resulted in determining and describing the five love languages. These love languages are easily distinguishable and based on Chapman's argument that if you use them successfully, your partner and the people around you will feel at ease. In turn, you will be comfortable as well.

Chapman states that every single person, everybody, has a primary love language. This is his or her love language mother tongue, the language through which he or she feels loved the most. It's no use for an American to try to talk to a German if they can't speak the other's language. The same applies to the love language exchange. Expecting someone to feel truly loved by "speaking" to her via a different love language is the same as expecting a German to understand English. Quite simply, they are unable to communicate with each other.

To ensure proper communication and full understanding of each other, it is a good idea to learn the other's love language. This book helps to decode the various ways in which couples communicate with one another, or generally how people interact, so we can finally understand what our significant other really wants from us. Learn about the preferences of others when it comes to receiving love. The rules apply to family relations, romantic relationships, and workplace relations as well. You can deal with other people better if you know their love language.

Not to mention the information stored in this book can help you to discover and understand your own love language too. Maybe you could never articulate what exactly you missed in your relationship, but you often felt your "love tank" was empty. With the help of the love languages you can tell your partner, your mother, or your friend how can they make you feel truly appreciated.

Words of affirmation: Showing your love and appreciation toward another person through words. Acknowledging their good deeds by telling them.

Quality time: Showing your love to someone by paying attention to them only. Your attention is not divided between your partner and your phone, computer, or TV. Give some time of your life just for them.

Gifts: Who doesn't like getting presents? But some of us like it more than others. Some regard it as an ineffective and empty gesture. Listen to them and try a different language with those people, as probably gifting is not their love language. But there are people who appreciate gifts more than your approving words or undivided attention.

Acts of service: Washing the dishes, giving good advice for work, or simply creating a quiet environment when your significant other or colleague wants to work are all acts of service. Their efficacy depends on the situation, and you will have to find the most appropriate way to apply them.

Physical touch: Many believe that this is the most intimate sphere of the love languages. Joy can be intensified and sorrow can be soothed by a simple touch, caress, or hug. Do you remember when you were a child how good it was to snuggle up to your mom or sit in your dad's lap? Every age has its own charm, in this respect. The tingling memory of a first hug or caress awakening your senses remains with everyone.

What's your love language? Find out by completing Gary Chapman's love language test at this link: http://www.5lovelanguages.com. If you understand and learn to use the five love languages, you have a higher chance of finding out what others value and therefore, how to connect with them the easiest way possible. You can also give hints to people how to please you the best way instead of sulking and waiting for them to figure it out.

The love language test will help to get to know yourself better. It will open up doors to you that you were not aware of before. Not many people analyze their needs in terms of "love languages," although they help a great deal in understanding your needs.

Have your partner, friends, and colleagues take the test as well. Keep the results of the tests and retake them quarterly or every six months. Compare the latest results with the previous ones. You will be surprised at how much your preferences can change in a year or two.

Keep in mind that just because you and your partner have a dominant love language doesn't mean you should stop "using" the other love languages. If strawberry is your favorite fruit, it doesn't mean you wouldn't eat an apple from time to time. The same goes for the love languages. Even though have a favorite one, you still enjoy experiencing the others as well.

Chapter 8: Imitate And Be Imitated

You have been using the easiest way of learning intuitively since you were a child: this is imitating. You copied everything people around you did. In the beginning, with limited success, but as time went by and you practiced more, you started to get the hang of it. Walking, talking, and value adaptation are all the results of imitation.

Knowledge is easier to obtain than to apply it to bear results. Sometimes you feel like you are sweating bullets while doing a task or finishing a job. You may think:

"How can others manage to do everything so easily? Why is it so hard for me?"

This is a legitimate question.

The assumption, however, that others do things easily is incorrect. Successful people have a lot of battle scars to show for what they have achieved. Only they know how many sleepless nights, failures, and attempts they experienced before they got their first reasonable result. How many times did they think, "This is enough, I don't want to struggle anymore"? But they closed their eyes and recalled their target and kept on going.

There is a roadside legend about Pablo Picasso. He was peacefully sitting and doodling on a napkin in a café in Madrid. When he finished his coffee, he crumpled the napkin-sketch and was about to throw it into the bin when a woman stopped him.

"You're Pablo Picasso, right? Can I have that napkin you drew on?"

"Sure," Picasso nodded unfolding the napkin. "It will be 20.000 dollars."

"What?" cried the woman. "You were just about to throw that away. It didn't take you more than two minutes to draw that, anyway."

"You're wrong. It took me forty years to draw this," said Picasso, and he walked away with the napkin.

There is hard work behind every great success. No great victory, accrual of money, or creation was achieved effortlessly. You can, however, ease your path with a simple trick. You knew this trick before you knew how to use a toilet. The trick is called imitation. If you want to explore a road that already has been explored, buy a map instead of re-discovering the globe from scratch.

Find those people who have great success in the area you want to explore. Read their books, seek their company and copy whatever you can from them. Don't be ashamed! If you get stuck, ask for their help, directly or indirectly. This doesn't mean you'll have to die being an imitator. But give yourself a head start. Achieve the standard goal quicker than the person who cleared the way. You will have plenty of time and opportunity to be original and add personal value to your goal when you're done with the known path. It doesn't make sense to re-invent the wheel, anyway. The wheel has already been invented. Use it to create something even better.

There is a very dangerous trap I want to warn you about. Steer clear of people who are conceited. This is a very dangerous emotion. This alone is enough to stop your progress. It is an obstacle in reaching your goal – whatever that goal is.

"If there are no appropriate conditions for your progress, then you need to create them!"

>What do you like to do?
>
>What are you good at?
>
>What do you need?

These are basic questions you need to answer to step on the path of self-realization. This word sounds pompous to me so I'll rephrase it. Do you remember the question you should ask yourself from Chapter 1? "What are the most important things for me to spend my time on?" As we've discussed, this is the better question to ask instead of "who am I?" and "what's my purpose?"

The three questions above will help you to answer this main, life-changing question:

"What are the most important things for me to spend my time on?"

It's ideal when your answers given to the three questions above overlap. For example, if you answered like the following, you're on board.

What do you like to do? — Exercise.

What are you good at? — Basketball.

What do you need? — More exercise in my life.

When only two of the three answers are similar, you are facing a situation for which a solution must be found. If they overlap to a small extent, it is worth further research. Do this until all three have common areas with the others, be they small or large.

Let's look at another sample of answers:

What do you like to do? — Exercise.

What are you good at? — Basketball.

What do you need? — Money.

Here there is an issue. Unless you can make money from playing basketball, you need to explore more possibilities, like becoming a commentator for basketball games, getting involved with your local sports community, founding and managing a local basketball team, and so on.

Be persistent and don't give up. The distance and difficulty of reaching their goal makes a lot of people give up even before crossing the starting line. You will take the first step. You can divide the distance into smaller portions so you will be able to do it. You might have to take on a bit more than what you find comfortable. Take on more and keep your commitments. Only then will you become stronger.

Don't talk yourself down during your journey. It will hold you back. Don't talk down others, either. Remember, awkward hurts. Don't judge people based on the vague information you have about them. Ask yourself:

What would I do if I were in their place?

It bothers you too if others belittle you.

Love obstacles because they show you what you are capable of when you overcome them. You become stronger by every trial where you stand tall. Pay attention to the signals from your environment. Learn to take advantage of them. It's no use to have talents, skills, abilities and knowledge if you don't utilize them.

Every day try to do a little more than the day before. So many people start out on a journey and give up before reaching their goal. They lose their faith, confidence and endurance on the long road. Don't give up on what you truly want. Maybe you just have to go a little further and success will be waiting for you right there. Keep the following "life wisdoms" in your mind on your journey:

- The eye is the mirror of the soul.

- A large man shows his size the way he treats smaller ones.

- "The deepest urge in human nature is the desire to be important." (John Dewey)

- The world is full of greedy and profit-seeking people. Whoever wants to selflessly help others can do it with almost no competition.

- You can get more friends in two months by being honestly interested in them than in five years if you just seek others who are interested in you.

- If you want to make friends, make an effort and offer help that requires time, energy, sacrifice and attention.

- Everyone is my master in what I can learn from him.

- "You cannot teach a man anything, you can only help him find it within himself." (Galileo Galilei)

- Do unto others, as you would have them do unto you.

- If you talk to someone about themselves they can pay attention for hours.

- A true friend is someone who knows you better than anyone, but still likes you.

- Take on tasks others have failed at, but do not hesitate to ask for help if you get stuck.

- Decide what you want to do and go for it.

- Time, effort and imagination are essential in getting ahead in life.

- Be the example you'd like to follow.

- Show your conversation partner respect by wanting to hear him out with an open mind.

- Those who love money will never have enough of it.

- Strive to get the most potential out of your capabilities.

- *Every idea is worth as much as you make of it.*

These are sayings of people who already walked a difficult path before you, and they experienced the accuracy of these lines. You can complete the list with your favorite "golden rules."

Chapter 9: Your Place In The World

In a monastery somewhere in Europe, a 9th-century monk entrusted with cooking put the lid on the cooking pot wrong. He put the pot over the hearth the night before and a curious frog somehow crawled into it. The fire was started the next morning and, as the temperature began to rise, the frog had adapted to the changing circumstances. It ended up on the plate of one of the monks.

They deliberated during breaks between prayers and decided to find out what exactly happened. The monks caught a few frogs in the pond and put one of them in the boiling water. The frog immediately jumped out of the pot and bolted from the scene of the scientific experiment. The second subject did likewise. They promptly slammed the lid on the third one and it was cooked in no time.

The next frog was put in cold water, and then the monks lit the fire underneath it. And what a surprise, the frog sat patiently at the bottom of the pot, calmly floating about even when the rising bubbles turned the water scalding hot. You could say that he happily swam to the netherworld. What came of the remains of this frog sacrificed in the pot of science is not written in the chronicles; only the conclusions gained from this event were presented in religious and scientific circles. They are still valid even in these days, and here they are:

- When you put a frog in cold water, his body will slowly adapt to the circumstances brought on by rising water temperatures.

- When the water temperature gets to be unbearably high, the frog will die; it won't have the energy to jump out of the pot because it already used it all up in the process of adapting.

Psychologists today like to use and apply this theory in their work. People can immediately react in a sudden emergency, run away, yell, kick, and bite and try to protect themselves in some way. When the threat is quiet and remote or bearable in intensity, then they try to adapt to it.

This is what happens when you:

- Work and make great efforts through being sick without taking time off

- Stay in toxic relationships

- Take care of something at work that you don't like, it's not your job or you don't get paid for

You endure the proverbial water that gets warmer and warmer by each burden you overtake, by each "no" you fail to say, by each person you sacrifice yourself for. Then when the water gets too hot, you will collapse. You can't jump out of it anymore because you used all your energy to adapt to the changing situation. You don't have any physical or mental strength left to jump out of the pot full of hot water, so you'll get cooked. This sounds morbid, but this is what happens to people who put others always first.

Easy adaptation is not a bad skill to have. The key is to recognize the right moment when to say no before you reach that critical point when you just feel totally cooked. This is the point when all your energy is gone and you are unable to make a good decision that could turn your ship toward a treasure island instead of a storm.

Learn from the mistakes of others. There is no shame in failure, in getting cooked a little bit, but it is unfortunate when you stay down, beaten, not even trying to get up.

Whatever happened, happened. Time to get up, my friend. I collected a few helpful ideas to you how to resist blind adaptation, be an attractive personality, and get out as a winner of the adversities life throws you in your way.

1. Let the other person start

We live in a human society. Often it is better to let the other person talk first. Let him talk and make him talk about his ideas, his life. Ask questions and try to get an idea of how he thinks, then try to come up with a conclusion for yourself. Learn from his mistakes and become more informed about others.

2. Affirm the other party

Steer clear of marginalized wording when it comes to controversial issues. Everyone has pride and ego can give bad advice.

A conversation should create mutual satisfaction. Try to avoid intense, black and white statements. "If you like it, we can continue, if not, then..." Or "I don't even want to talk about this" remark won't bring results or would make it very difficult to come to an agreement.

3. Empathy

Put yourself in the other person's place. Perhaps ask yourself some questions pertaining to the situations and answer them in the other party's place. This method can reveal that the other person might not be on the same page with you but that doesn't mean he's wrong.

4. Avoid traps and ask back

When you feel that something is wrong, someone is asking unpleasant questions or the conversation is taking a wrong turn, you should ask "What do you base this on?" or "Why did you say that?" This question might mitigate the harshness of your answer or might make the other party think about their own position or attitude. In addition, while they respond you have time to think.

5. Listen

If someone simply ignores the other's comments, it will have bad consequences. Lasting relationships are not built on good communication skills but rather on good listening skills.

6. Emotional adjustments

Emotions are an important building block of relationship cultivation. Uncover the other party's emotional state when you engage in a conversation. When you adjust your talking style to the other party's mood, you'll have a better chance at engaging in a meaningful conversation. For example, if someone's clearly sad, don't start by talking about your awesome life. If someone is happy, don't hit a melodramatic tone.

7. Be honest

Honesty is a very strong skill. If you use it well, it will clear the road for you, and even the seemingly impossible can become reality. Figure out a few honest sentences tailored to your personality and practice them in conversations, like: "In my opinion …" or "I'm very hopeful that …"

8. Stay on target

Everybody values their time. You value your time, as well. When you engage in conversation with a specific reason, stay on the target topic as much as possible. Be concise and straightforward. People appreciate no nonsense communication, especially in business.

9. Don't complain

You must have heard from people the following things, "We are cursed. We can never succeed. Whatever we do is wrong. "

Few people are able to accept without complaint the slaps of life, because it's easier to find excuses than to look for the reasons, which have been triggering that particular thing. Most people start their working life on a path that is rather a necessity than desire. Whatever you choose to follow, you're responsible for your decision. Complaints won't improve your life.

Final Words

In a historical novel I read the following word: "Porphyrogenitus." The initial meaning, according to Wikipedia, is "an honorific title in the Byzantine Empire given to a son or daughter born after the father had become emperor."[iv] I started thinking about the deeper meaning of this word and its interpretation in the present age. Who would be today's Porphyrogenitus? Is somebody Porphyrogenitus who:

- Is the kid of wealthy parents?

- The child of parents with political power?

- The child of a known public figure like an actor?

- A famous athlete's child?

- A child who comes from parents who are known for their scientific work?

- Or simply a child who saw the light of day in a family, where parents have a health-oriented approach to life? A child who is disciplined, purposeful and steadily progressing toward their life goals?

You may also refine the approach, although here the focus is on the family-offered circumstances that create the opportunity for a good life. Even for those who are born into advantageous circumstances, only a fraction are able to take advantage of family background.

Who loves water? And who can swim? How did you start learning to swim? What was the feeling when you first floated atop the water and did not sink in? How did you learn the arm and leg movements? Who learned the breathing technique easily? Why did you want to learn to swim — to enjoy the water, or to swim through a lake or a river?

And if you choose to cross the Atlantic? It's better to use a ship for that. Whether you have smaller dreams like to learning to swim in shallow water, or you have great dreams of traveling the seven seas, you'll need a map, an instruction guide. Your map is a teacher — a mentor if you like.

But who's a good teacher? Would you choose a man who's only read or heard about swimming or sailing? Maybe he has seen it on TV, but never tried it? Or would you choose a master who knows all the ins and outs of swimming and sailing and is able to teach you too? What kind of knowledge, practice, and perseverance would you need to take your dream to the finish line?

"What would a person who can solve this task do in my place?" — Address this question to yourself.

Search for the teacher who will help you realize your ideas and dreams. A teacher shows you how you can turn a hypothetical situation into reality. If you are stuck somewhere, a teacher helps you move on. When you reach a crossroad, he or she shows you how to decide which is the correct direction for you. Your teacher not only helps you to do your job well, but also to live a better life.

Remember, the rest of your life is still in front of you. You can do anything you want with it.

I really believe in you!

Yours truly,

Zoe

P.S.: If you have questions please don't hesitate to contact me on **zoemckey@gmail.com**. I welcome any kind of constructive opinion as well. I'd like to know how I can help so please share your ideas with me. If you'd like to get helpful tips from me on a weekly basis, visit me at **www.zoemckey.com** and subscribe. Thank you!

Epilogue

Here you can find the more detailed description of the four temperament types. The history of the four temperament types goes back to the ancient Greco-Roman times. The Greek Hippocrates included these types into his medical theories.

Sanguine Type

Extrovert/Talkative/Optimistic

People with sanguine temperament are cheerful, confident and optimistic. They like to sing in the shower, and they use exclamation points after every sentence! They have nicknames for their close friends. In general, they are the life of the party. At work, sanguine people inspire and motivate others to do the job.

Strengths

Their personality is very pleasant, and people like to hang out with them. They have good stories and never run out of things to say. The party is where they are. They have a good sense of humor and love to be with people. They wear their emotions on their sleeve. They have many interests. They are honest and maybe a little gullible. They do volunteer work. They are always coming up with new things to do, and they are creative and colorful. They always make a good impression and like to create flashy intros for the programs they are entrusted with. They are enthusiastic and love people. They can successfully persuade others to join them. They love compliments and spontaneous things. They don't hold a grudge, and they ask for forgiveness immediately.

Weaknesses

They tend to let current conditions govern their lives. They exaggerate and never run out of words. The often don't remember people's names, but they can talk endlessly about trivial things. Complacent and naïve. They can get angry quickly and are very loud. Some find them too happy and superficial. They are restless, you can't count on them and they live for the present. They are slackers; they'd rather talk than work. They forget their obligations and are disorganized. They make their decisions based on their emotions and can easily be distracted. It is hard for them to finish what they start and they easily lose their confidence. They don't plan for the future. They hate being alone and can't handle when they are not the center of attention. They feed off of popularity and recognition. They dominate others in discussions, cut them off and don't pay attention to what the others have to say. They like to talk for others. They repeat their stories and jokes several times. They are very good at making excuses for themselves. In relationships, their friendliness can be ambiguous their interest may seem more serious than it is.

Choleric Type

Extrovert/Active/Optimistic

The name comes from the word cholera (bile, anger). In the Middle Ages the bile was considered to be the starting point of anger. Although this personality type is quick-tempered, they can still be best described as well-prepared and disciplined. In general, they are motivated, self-starters and hard workers. Choleric people get over the difficulties of life and accomplish a lot. At work choleric people overcome obstacles and successfully perform tasks.

Strengths

They are strong-minded, confident and courageous. Very active. They are born leaders and call it like they see it. They are reliable and responsible, and they never postpone things. They are tough and persistent. They set goals and accomplish them. They are dynamic, active and have an instinctive need for change. They have a need to right the wrongs. They are independent and not easily discouraged. Not emotional. They exude confidence and there is nothing they can't lead. They work hard for the success of the team. In general, they can understand the situation and are dazzling in emergency situations. They see the whole point and get into it quickly. Purposeful and organized. They are always looking for practical solutions and can distribute work well. They can get everyone moving and love challenges.

Weaknesses

Impatient and can suddenly fly into a rage. They are bossy and it is difficult for them to encourage others. They are insensitive and power through others, especially when they are stressed. They have a sharp tongue. They focus on things to do instead of relationships. Not willing to quit an argument even when they are wrong. It is hard for them to relax, and they have a strong a presence. Inflexible and unable to tolerate mistakes. They are always in a hurry. They can be rude and disrespectful.

They manipulate people for their own benefit. Hate tears and sentimentality. In fact, out of the different areas of their lives, their emotions are the least developed. Trivial information bores them. They don't like thinking about details so they make frantic decisions sometimes. They have high expectations towards others. They live according to "the end justifies the means" rule. They can be obsessed with their work. They demand endless loyalty from their friends, their subordinates. In relationships, they tend to dominate the other and be very jealous. It is difficult for them to recognize their mistakes and they hardly ever apologize. They feel they can make decisions best, so they decide for everybody. They also believe they do everything better than everybody else, so they just do it all. They feel they don't need many friends.

Melancholic Type

Introvert/Thinker/Pessimistic

The original meaning of the word is sad, gloomy, moody, but it has changed to meditative and deep thinking today. Melancholic people can be characterized by high degrees of diligence and seriousness. They like to be alone, and they enjoy silence. They are very emotion-oriented, and their feelings can reach ecstasy levels or can push them to despair. They like to take time to look at one thing from several points of view. They like to join others, but they are not pushy, and they like it when other people take the initiative. At work, people who are melancholic are in charge of good quality and creative solutions.

Strengths

People who are characterized by being melancholic are insightful, sensitive and conscientious. They are very intense, serious and resolute. They have a tendency for genius, are talented and very creative. Philosophical and idealistic. They value and enjoy beauty in all forms. They are very loyal, sensitive to others and communicate well. They are self-sacrificing, precise and analytical. Pedantic in their work, they organize their things well and are self-disciplined. They are soft-spoken and pleasant people who are usually gifted in arts, poetry and music. They raise the bar high and are persistent. They like schedules, are penny-pinchers and like order. It is easy for them to recognize problems, inconsistencies and find creative solutions for them. They like tables, formulas and illustrations. They finish what they start. They feel comfortable in the background, and they don't like to draw attention to themselves. They are loyal friends and listen to what the other person is saying; deeply sympathize with others.

Weaknesses

Melancholic are often moody and depressed. Prone to poor self-image and self-loathing. They are preoccupied with themselves and dream a lot. It is difficult for them to forgive and forget. They are only satisfied with perfection, so it is hard to meet their needs. They often feel guilty about small things. There are times when they think others don't like them and they tend to be hypochondriacs. They are very cautious about making new friends and are looking for the perfect partner. They can get depressed when they discover an imperfection, a blemish in themselves or others. They do not initiate; they spend too much time thinking. Their emotions determine the quality of their work. They have a great need for encouragement, acceptance. Socially insecure, shy and distant. It is difficult to get to know them because they are very aloof. It is hard for them to take compliments. They tend to criticize others. They are vengeful, can be obnoxious. They are full of contradictions.

Phlegmatic Type

Perceiver/Pessimistic

People who are phlegmatic are relaxed, calm and often seem without emotions. They are very difficult to motivate or to launch into action. They like doing things that don't require a lot of energy, for example, reading, watching TV, doing crossword puzzles, etc. They are positive and calm even in distressing situations. They are passive at social events, because they are more comfortable watching people than actively participating in conversations. At work, they are renowned for their cooperation.

Strengths

Phlegmatic are diplomatic people; their presence is calming and desired in stressful situations. They are delightful and sympathetic. They get along with a lot of different people. Competent, constant and talented in administrative tasks. They are quiet, calm, relaxed and balanced. They are compassionate, kind. Good at interceding and keeping the peace. Perform well under pressure. They pay attention to others during conversations. They like to find the simplest, easiest solutions. They have good people skills and have a lot of friends. They are patient and accepting. Have a dry sense of humor and are easy to be with. They are natural and chaste.

Weaknesses

A phlegmatic weakness is that they often lack motivation, they are lazy and apathetic. It is difficult for them to make a decision and they are prone to selfishness. Neglectfulness is another trait of theirs, so they might seem careless, cold and might make us feel like that they don't like us. At times, they may watch too much TV and are more spectators than participants of life. They avoid confrontation and there are times when they make compromises they cannot keep just to have peace. They are passive rebels, and they exclude what they don't like. They can be depressing, fearful and hesitant. They avoid responsibilities and are too restrained. Self-justified and don't like to set goals for themselves. They hate it when they must do things. They are opposed to change and are neutral towards plans of others. They like to criticize and tease others, can have a sharp tongue. It is hard to get to know them, because they are not vulnerable, hide their emotions and avoid difficult situations. They always pick the easiest, least energy-intensive path.

Link to the temperament description and test from Chapter 6 and the Epilogue:
http://www.tulelocsomag.hu/cikkek/1052vermersekletteszt.html
http://psychologia.co/four-temperaments/

Osborn L. Ac., David K. *INHERENT TEMPERAMENT*. Retrieved. 2013.

Reference

Ferenc Margitics, Zsuzsa Pauwlik. *Vocational Eligibility of Pedagogue Candidates in Respect of Temperament and Characteristics*. Department of Psychology, College of Nyíregyháza, Hungary. 2004. http://real.mtak.hu/5120/1/1136932.pdf

LaHaye, Tim. *Your Temperament: Discover Its Potential*. Tyndale Publishing. 1984.

Manson, Mark. *Procrastination*. Mark Manson. 2015. https://markmanson.net/procrastination

Osborn L. Ac., David K. *INHERENT TEMPERAMENT*. Retrieved. 2013.

Psychologia. *Four Temperaments: Sanguine, Phlegmatic, Choleric, and Melancholic Personality Types.* Psychologia. http://psychologia.co/four-temperaments/

Túlélőcsomag. *Vérmérséklet teszt*. Túlélőcsomag. 2009. http://www.tulelocsomag.hu/cikkek/1052vermersekletteszt.html

Wikipedia. *Porphyrogennetos.* Wikipedia. 2010. https://en.wikipedia.org/wiki/Porphyrogennetos

More Books By Zoe

Discipline Your Mind

Find What You Were Born For – Book 1

Find What You Were Born For – Book 2

Catching Courage

Fearless

Daily Routine Makeover

Daily Routine Makeover – Evening Edition

Morning Routine Makeover

Less Mess Less Stress

Braver Than You Believe

The Unlimited Mind

Wired For Confidence

Minimalist Makeover

Build Social Confidence

Communication and Confidence Coaching

By working with me you can expect to gain a better understanding of yourself, and the hope you need to change your life for the better. I will help you understand everybody around you better starting with yourself. My three main goals are to help you:

- Embrace discomfort to break down your negative beliefs,
- Find your strengths and focus on them,
- Bring out the side of you that is totally comfortable with yourself and your environment.

I have a unique approach to coaching. The entire lesson is composed of two parts:

Interpersonal Skills Development

Do your palms sweat and your heart pound when you enter in a room full of strangers? Do you feel awkward when somebody starts a conversation with you? Do you fear you'll run out of things to say and wish you could just talk casually with everybody?

Then this course was made for you!

In this section, I'll help you learn how to communicate with others, how to be presentable, and how to always make a great impression. Humans are social beings and since you live among them you can never underestimate the importance of social skills. If you have them you can be 100-percent present and aware in any situation. I have been studying and developing communication and real-life social interaction skills for more than 10 years. I've written 10 books – all of them Amazon best-sellers – on the topic. I can help you, please let me!

Here you will learn:

- How to start conversations and keep them going with anybody,
- How to "win friends and influence people,"
- Airy, pleasant ways to be more charming and likable,
- How to be the life of the party, and
- Tips on how to handle difficult conversations and people.

I'll teach you how to be the person everyone notices when you enter the room, the person who instantly sparks people's interest and can talk easily to anyone.

Intrapersonal Skills Development

Is the mirror your worst enemy? Or the scale? Or both? Do you feel uncomfortable with who you are? Do you sometimes feel your days are passing by without any purpose? Is sleeping your favorite activity? Do you wish you were somewhere else, maybe someone else?

If any of these statements apply to you then you have work to do. Living with self-contempt, regrets, and frustration is not sustainable. In this part of the coaching I will help you to accept and recover from any inner struggles you have. With honesty and commitment, I will guide you to let go of old wounds, and help you find your strengths and develop them in order to bring out the best in yourself.

I'll help you:

- to discover the root cause of your problems,
- recover from childhood traumas,
- communicate with yourself objectively and silence the malicious voices in your head,
- build confidence and self-respect, and learn to be persistent and get what you want.

If you're interested, apply here:

http://www.zoemckey.com/contact/

Endnotes

---

[i] Read more about this idea in Simon Sinek's *Start With Why* book.

[ii] Ferenc Margitics, Zsuzsa Pauwlik. *Vocational Eligibility of Pedagogue Candidates in Respect of Temperament and Characteristics*. Department of Psychology, College of Nyíregyháza, Hungary. 2004. http://real.mtak.hu/5120/1/1136932.pdf

[iii] Manson, Mark. *Procrastination*. Mark Manson. 2015. https://markmanson.net/procrastination

[iv] Wikipedia. *Porphyrogennetos*. Wikipedia. 2010. https://en.wikipedia.org/wiki/Porphyrogennetos

www.ingramcontent.com/pod-product-compliance
Lightning Source LLC
Chambersburg PA
CBHW020105240426
43661CB00002B/42